Since You Didn't Ask

A Collection of Life's Avoidable Pitfalls

© 2019 Christopher Page

Published by: Ingram Spark Publishing

Editorial and Production: Ms. Allaneous
Editor: Helena Handbasket
Type design and cover art: Amanda Reckonwith

All rights reserved. This book may not be reproduced in whole or in part, or transmitted in any form, or by any means electronic, mechanical, photocopying, recording, or other, without written permission from the publisher, except by a reviewer who may quote brief passages in a review.

Library of Congress Cataloging-in-Publication Data

Page, Christopher
Since You Didn't Ask
A Collection of Life's Avoidable Pitfalls

ISBN Print: 978-0-578-55830-1
ISBN Epub: 978-0-578-55826-4

Printed in the U.S.A.

Acknowledgements

To my Wife, Robin,
Daughter, Hannah and my Son, Nicholas

"Wealth may be an excellent thing, for it means power, it means leisure, it means liberty"
~ *James Russell Lowell*

Contents:
Forward

Section 1
The three human behaviors
1. Control
2. Ownership
3. Modification

Section 2
Behave like a poor person
4. Focus on doubt
5. Compare yourself to others
6. Have a fear of success
7. Blame your bad childhood
8. Stay in your comfort zone
9. Talk down to yourself
10. Keep your house messy
11. Money doesn't buy happiness
12. Shoot for that one big break
13. Don't quit your day job
14. Give up everything for your kids
15. Act desperate
16. Get hustled
17. Take things personally
18. Please everyone
19. There are no stupid questions
20. Hate your job
21. Carry a credit card balance
22. Borrow money from relatives
23. Get into a partnership with a friend
24. Keep lousy records
25. Be a flake
26. Never give up
27. Follow Your Passion
28. Be all you can be

Section 3
Hate the Corporation
- 29. It's lonely at the top
- 30. Mix business relationships
- 31. Get bound by time
- 32. Be a team player
- 33. My company can't get by without me
- 34. Do your own accounting
- 35. Walk into a negotiation with no options
- 36. The customer is always right

Section 4
You and business narcissism
- 37. "I" want to start "my" own business
- 38. Sell products and services you like
- 39. Sell cheap junk
- 40. Offer services that nobody wants to pay for
- 41. Build a dam and hope for rain
- 42. Throw money at a business to get it to happen

Section 5
Yak it up to the wrong people
- 43. Incessantly share with others
- 44. Hang out with losers
- 45. Toil endlessly with another person's "Venue"
- 46. Hang out with evil, condescending control freaks
- 47. Tell everyone about your current lawsuit
- 48. Answer questions and explain yourself
- 49. Attempt to prove your worthiness
- 50. Blab to people at work
- 51. Share your mistakes
- 52. Tell everyone you're an expert
- 53. Tell the world you found a bag of money
- 54. Argue with people who are impossible
- 55. Help other people first

Backward

Forward...

I'm going to give you a country to rule...

Your country has an ocean port, a river, beautiful mountains and open farmland. Your country also has citizens. What are you going to do with your country and your citizens? Your citizens will need to be educated so the country will function. Your society will need some doctors, a few lawyers, civil engineers, mechanics, programmers, teachers, laborers, farmers, etc. To create this workforce, you will need to set up a school system. Your school system will offer basics of knowledge, as well as create discipline and focus for the people.

There is a name for this process – it is called social engineering. Without social engineering, one would end up with a country filled to capacity with uneducated toothless peasants. Since modern societies need a workforce, we are taught in school to be employees by being treated like employees. We get to class at 8:00 a.m., take a lunch, leave at 3:00 p.m., then do our homework and don't ask questions. Were you ever asked if you wanted to work for someone else or work for yourself? You weren't. Did you ever see *Real Estate Mogul 101* in your college course book? How about a major in *Chief Executive Officer*? Sorry, not there. You cannot create a social hierarchy if you teach all of your citizens to be financially independent. To teach citizens an early path to financial independence would create an unmanageable country with all Chiefs and no Indians. We must be taught mediocrity by the school system, or our corporations won't be delivered any employees.

Compulsory schooling does not, and cannot teach independence. Societies need scores of scurrying workers, not an army of millionaires. To create this workforce, you must create the *need* to work. If you teach your citizens to be independent, they won't need to work, and you won't have a workforce. If a big business handed the year's profits to its employees, the employees would lose their will to work. The old "rich get richer and the poor get poorer" doctrine must exist or the economy would fall into chaos.

At the risk of sounding onerous, the key to maintaining a viable, functioning social hierarchy is maintaining fear. We citizens must be afraid of loss of income to obey orders. As employees we are taught to have one income and work to create a savings, invest in stocks, etc. On the other hand, corporations start multiple projects, dump the ones that don't work, create multiple incomes, and work to create power through positive income investments and diversification of cash flow. To achieve this success, you must think like and operate like a big business, don't think like an employee or a student.

The correct move is to diversify, not your investments, but your cash flow opportunities. Consider all types of income, from traditional employment to rental property and small business. The best time to start down this road is today. You will need five years of experience in almost any field before it's viable. The day after you get laid off is a bad time to go back to school to be a _____.

Entire towns are guilty of falling victim to the single income mentality. I have lost track of the number of times I have heard of Hometown USA collapsing when the steel mill or automobile plant closes. One business goes belly up and the whole town disintegrates. Multiple incomes are the key to survival for big business, towns, cities, and you.

> "Only people who die very young learn all they really need to know in kindergarten"
> ~*Wendy Kaminer*

Section 1
The three human behaviors

I see what you're getting at Johnson, but I feel like we're getting into a grey area.

What we do . . .

We like to give ourselves lots of credit. I refer to humans in general. Written language, space travel, opposing thumbs, etc. We are grotesquely impressed with ourselves. When it comes to our existence, we wash every action through three definitions of behavior. These three levels of influence and inference infect everything we do. The magic three are; control, ownership, and modification.

1. Control

The first human behavior above all else is control. Who's in charge - that's the first order of business. Consider a government. Any government. From federal down to state to the school board to children deciding who plays what position on a football team. It's all filtered through the question of *who is in charge*. We are all about power. Think for a moment the words that are used surrounding the very concept of power. The U.S. Air *Force* is not the U.S. Air *Suggestion*. Would you yield power to the Police recommendation department?

There are an incessant slew of power words we grind through our lives without questioning. Think of these words, they come up constantly, and we bow to them: *permit; allow; let; approve; tolerate, etc*. Even something as simple as missing a day of work. In many cases employers require a note from a doctor. Approval from elsewhere is the conceptual definition of the law. We like to imagine the law "keeps us safe", but it actually keeps us in line.

The very concept of government has to do with power. "The Law" is the transfer of power from the individual to a manifestation of collective consciousness which we call government. Cynical opinion, but true. When we like to refer to the law, what we are really saying is "you as an individual do not have the right to make that decision". If all the decision making power rested with the individual, that is called *anarchy,* like the Wild Wild West in the 1800's. The antithesis of anarchy is a *totalitarian dictatorship* like North Korea or California.

Power is money. Wealth is personal power. Wealthy people can make more decisions about daily activities than those who are always strapped for cash. Being broke is a process of being controlled by perpetual failure. The more money you have the more power you have over your destiny. Money is power. Corny, but true. The more power you have to make decisions the more fun life is. I bought a car I've always wanted a little while back. Lots of fun.

"If you lie down so people can walk all over you they will still complain you are not flat enough"
~ Anonymous

2. Ownership

The second thing that humans do is decide who owns what. My house, my car, my money, my dog. Don't touch my stuff. This is also the second thing our government does after deciding who is in charge, they track ownership. All governments have terrifying mountains of information regarding ownership of almost all of your possessions. These volumes of records conveniently spill over into the concept of taxes and how much tax they can levy against that ownership. You own it, they keep track of it and tax it. In fact, the oldest type of tax in history is *personal ownership tax* or property tax. Sales and income tax are relatively new concepts, both types have only been around for a hundred years. On the other hand, levying of tax on personal property goes back hundreds if not thousands of years.

Taxation aside, increasing your personal ownership of any desirable asset comes with the power to make decisions and be in control. The concept of ownership and power go together. The more you own of something the more power you have to make decisions with respect to that asset. If you owe a ton of money on a car, or a large percentage of the value, and you miss a payment, the bank takes the car. If you owned 100% of the car, you would by definition control the whole car. Same with real estate. The concept of real estate ownership goes beyond single person or entity ownership, but may include splitting the property into percentages of ownership among multiple parties. You can own part of a house, or part of a piece of land. This fact folds back into control. The percentage you own is the percentage you control. If you have a mortgage get rid of it as fast as possible. Don't keep a mortgage to get the tax break. That's a stupid reason. When you own the house, you are in control.

Here is the key to ownership and power. Ownership, power and control only exist if you possess something that somebody else wants. This point is so important I am going to repeat it: *ownership, power and control only exist if you possess something that somebody else wants*. If you own it and nobody wants it, you have no power.

I mean honestly, why in the world do diamonds have value? Diamonds are stupid. They don't do anything. You can make record needles out of them I suppose, but aside from that people want them because they are rare and sparkly. So, other than basic needs such as water, food and shelter, *desire to possess* drives value. If you own a desired asset, you by definition have power.

> "And I would argue the second greatest force
> in the universe is ownership".
> ~ *Chris Chocola*

3. Modification

The third human behavior once one has secured control and ownership is modification. We buy then control cars, houses, motorcycles, or anything we like to possess or own. After that we change it. Make a better one. Paint it a different color. Buy property and build something on it. Install a bigger engine. Humans are the modifiers. Many years ago school textbooks cited man as being different than his earthbound animal co-inhabitants because man was the toolmaker or the *modifier*. We could take some object from the environment, change it, and make it into something else. This tale held true until we witnessed primates and some bird species like crows modifying items from the environment and using them for a specific purpose. So much for man the toolmaker. We had to switch the "we are special" song to "our brain is bigger". Most whale species and some land animals like elephants have larger brains than we do, so I suppose we will have to change the subject again.

Nevertheless, we are the modifiers. We change what others have done and put our spin on it. We cut down trees and build houses. We dig up metal and make cars.

We also grind trees up to make paper so we can have an opinion and write a book.

"Change is the law of life -
those who look only to the past or present
are certain to miss the future."
~ *John F. Kennedy*

Section 2
Behave like a poor person

4. Focus on doubt

When you doubt yourself, you generate negative energy that permeates the fiber of the Universe. There is no scientific evidence for this effect; however, when you feel good about yourself things magically come together. On the other hand, if you incessantly mistrust your world, the facts mirror the feelings. Perpetual failure inextricably accompanies doubt.

Success is a perception. You need to be convinced you're worthy, or you won't be. Other people instantly perceive feelings of inadequacy like a dog smells fear, so to succeed at anything, you need to maintain a sense of entitlement. Power and freedom must exist in the mind before they exist anywhere else. As with success, authority is also a perception. In fact, the President is only the President because we think he is. He has to think he is, too.

"Perpetual optimism is a force multiplier"
~ *Colin Powell*

5. Compare yourself to others

Someone always has a bigger house or a better car, so ignore envy forever. Money, wealth and success really boil down to how you feel about your own existence, and have nothing to do with comparisons. Constantly keeping up with the Joneses is a loosing battle on any front, so concentrate on planning your own game then playing it.

> "We forfeit three-fourths of ourselves in order
> to be like other people"
> ~ *Arthur Schopenhaur (1788 – 1860)*

6. Have a fear of success

The idiotic psychobabble "fear of success" claim is quite simply a bad excuse for being a chicken. Nobody is afraid of succeeding, and nobody is afraid of being praised for achievements. When you begin making $250,000 a year, you will adjust to this situation very quickly. Before you launch a business that will require spending or moving large sums of money, write a big practice check. Write it for $25,000 and look at it. You may never have seen one. Not so scary, once you've done it.

"Fear of success" is just as ridiculous as "alcoholism is a disease." Is cigarette smoking a disease? Was I born with the Marlboro gene? These claims simply remove personal guilt from bad behavior.

You're not afraid of failure a hundred times, or even five hundred times, because these are comfortable, finite numbers. What you're really afraid of is working on something for years and having it never go anywhere. You're not afraid of *finite failure*, you're afraid of *total failure*.

Here is what happens in your mind after an initial disappointment, so get ready. The brick wall you have encountered gives rise to an angry, hollow, black hole of terror that is fueled by the realization that the concept you have set in motion may never happen. Ignore this vacant fear and press on. Concern yourself with the task at hand. Work on today. Triumphs are not singular, they add up as you go.

> "The greatest mistake you can make in life is to be continually fearing you'll make one"
> *~ Elbert Hubbard (1856-1915)*

7. Blame your bad childhood

Oh, boo hoo. Timmy Ferguson stole my lunch money. Everyone had a bad childhood. You likely cannot go back to Timmy and get him to apologize, so the horizon is a better place to look than your yearbook without enough signatures. Become an architect. Write a book. Go to the beach. The football captain in High School usually ends up a gasket salesman in Poughkeepsie anyway, so pull your socks up and move on.

"Living well is the best revenge"
~ *George Herbert (1593-1633)*

8. Stay in your comfort zone

Doing the same thing over and over while expecting different results is a formula for permanent failure. Personal comfort zones involve familiar quantities and parameters; everything else is unknown and worrisome. Get used to the unknown, it's the only way to get anywhere.

There's this funny thing that happens when you strike out on your own. You get scared of the telephone. You will notice this phenomenon when you start your own business and the phone rings for the first time. Answering the phone at your old job was really easy, but answering *your own* business line will be like getting a root canal. Unsuccessful people avoid this mini hurdle because it makes them uncomfortable. Get used to doing things that make you nervous, the jump is shorter than you think.

We have all seen friends and acquaintances turn down opportunities for seemingly plausible, but ultimately odd reasons. The opportunity was likely avoided due to a bizarre fear of accepting success. You may have done this yourself without realizing it, bolstering the decision to pass with handy excuses.

Attempt the unfamiliar. Being uncomfortable becomes comfortable as you continually pursue the unknown. Breaking out of your comfort zone is a little like gambling. Don't bet the pile and don't test the depth of the water with both feet. But do place the bet, just not the same way every time.

> "A mind once expanded by a new idea never regains its original dimensions"
> *~ Oliver Wendell Holmes*

9. Talk down to yourself

"I never was very good at spelling" or "I'm terrible with money" or any other iteration of self-putdown will serve to keep you right where you are. If you find you are putting yourself down, go look in the mirror and repeat the phrase. See what others see when you're disrespectful to number one.

This type of verbal failure reinforcement is not only destructive; it will become a habit. When you insist on galvanizing problems with your own harsh words, problems are what you will seek, and problems are what you will have.

"Choose your words carefully…they guide the mind"
~ *Louise Herald (My wise grandmother)*

10. Keep your house messy

Houses are either kept clean or kept messy – both situations are a decision. Messy houses are perfect excuses for failure. Very few millionaires live in filthy homes. I'm sure one could conger up a handy story of some weird, wiry haired mumbling millionaire living in a trash filled mansion, but this is far from the norm. If you really want success, clean the garage, sell off the bric-a-brac, and immediately dump the self-storage unit. A messy house is a messy mind. As soon as the house is presentable, you will have more money…just like magic.

> "Cleanliness and order are not matters of instinct; they are matters of education, and like most great things, you must cultivate a taste for them."
> ~ *Benjamin Disraeli*

11. Money doesn't buy happiness

Yes it does. This phrase is a lame excuse used by people who don't have any. Whenever the subject of money comes up, some imbecile always says, "I know a lot of unhappy rich people". So what. *Everyone* who is broke is unhappy, so I'll be rich and take my chances. Money gives you the freedom to pursue other ventures, gain respect, go on fun vacations and have peace of mind. You'll be happier with it than without it.

"With money in your pocket, you are wise, you are handsome and you sing well, too"
~ Chinese proverb

12. Shoot for that one big break

Yes, it's happened. Bolt of lightning success has come to a very few. However, most successful people got to where they are with sandpaper, not with a saw. We often hold a lottery-like expectation for success. This "lotteryesque" perception of a breakthrough is attractive for two reasons. First, we like the instant money concept. Second, we want to skip what we know to be true: success is a process requiring the building of knowledge and experience. There will be a day where everything will come together, but this will be followed by years of it not.

Encouraging phrases like "shoot for the moon", "go for it" and "think big" are fun and everything, but decidedly campy and unrealistic. We all want to go from zero to a hundred miles an hour in an instant. First consider resources that are within reach. Yes, you would like to build a skyscraper, but you will probably have to start with a doghouse. You could build a skyscraper shaped doghouse I suppose, but that will have to be the starting point. Then build a guesthouse, then a three bedroom two and a half bath, and then maybe an apartment building.

Things in business happen about as quickly as roots lifting a sidewalk. The key is steady pressure. Don't shelve any idea you are actively pursuing, the energy gets cold. The key is not working until midnight for one day, but to keep steady pressure all week, two hours at a time. Accomplish something every day. Do not skip a day, because then you will skip a week. Then a week will become a month, a year, etc.

The first attempt at anything always takes the most time. This is due to the fact that you may not have the experience, and therefore are searching for the right parts to the puzzle and the order in which to assemble them. The first time out, learn to enjoy your ignorance. Find intrigue in the void and move forward, even though the only information you obtain is that you were going in the wrong direction.

By all means set goals, make plans and work towards them. However, shoot for the attainable rather than the moon. It is far better to have a hundred small successes than one huge failure. It's fun to aspire to be an astronaut, but learning to fly a biplane is quite an accomplishment, rightly considered.

> "It takes twenty years of hard work
> to become an overnight success"
> *~ Diana Rankin*

13. Don't quit your day job

You should consider quitting your day job. Most other businesses are open from nine to five, so it just makes sense to be available during that time. There are some positions where the shift starts at 5:00 a.m. and end at noon, and some start at 2:30 p.m. and end at 10:30 p.m. Both of these allow flexible time during the workday to pursue other ventures. It's very difficult to get things off the ground when you don't have any time to make a phone call.

"Work only a half a day. It makes no difference which half, the first 12 hours or the last 12 hours"
~ Kemmons Wilson –
Founder of the Holiday Inn hotel chain

14. Give up everything for your kids

We all love our children, but this is your life, too. How are you going to set an example for your children if you never accomplish anything? I realize we've all heard this story, but there was a woman I knew whose parents immigrated to the United States years ago. They didn't speak English, and had no money when they arrived. They opened a grocery store. They worked at the grocery store twelve hours a day, seven days a week. No vacations, and no days off. They had literally given up everything for their kids. When it came time for this young girl to go to college, all she had ever been exposed to was the inside of a grocery store. She had no experiences to draw on. No vacations, no breaks. She had no life experience to help her make a decision.

When your children have children should they also give up everything? Why bother giving everything up for your children if they are just going to have to forgo their success for their offspring? How many generations are going to pass before someone has a life? If you want your children to excel, then you must strive to excel.

"Children have never been very good at listening to their elders, but they have never failed to imitate them"
~ *James Baldwin*

15. Act Desperate

Here's the road to the top. Be desperate and needy. Over the top eagerness is a sure fire way to get familiar with the sidewalk. Chief executive officers are generally cool as a cucumber. Donald Trump has lost $250,000 in an afternoon and somehow he shrugged it off. That's not to say that losing $250,000 isn't irritating, but the fact that he can take the loss in stride makes him fascinating.

Be cool. Be measured. Act as if you've got a secret. Act like you've got a lot of money. Just don't talk about it. Behave like this before you have the secret or the money so you'll be ready when you do.

"An unhurried sense of time is in itself a form of wealth"
~ Bonnie Friedman

16. Get Hustled

If you are looking for a sure fire way to get screwed, let yourself get hustled. As soon as you start to feel the walls of speed start to close in on a deal, step back and take a look around. When you're buying the "last one" or the "sale ends at midnight tonight" you're on your way to purchasing a lump of coal. Successful business deals are made methodically. Once the money changes hands, backing up is nearly impossible. Why someone is getting rid of something is far more important than why you are buying it.

"Half our life is spent trying to find something to do with the time we have rushed through life trying to save"
~ *Will Rogers*

17. Take Things Personally

Feel small and puny, that's a great idea. Powerful real estate developers who felt rejected, sad and depressed are responsible for constructing many of the buildings in New York City. Greatness is often achieved by feeling put upon and left out.

Get used to rejection. It's part of life as well as business. I suppose you could rush to the psychiatrist's office and secure a prescription for an anti rejection medication every time your feelings get hurt, but let's get serious. If you are writing a book, for example, you will be rejected hundreds of times. If you get puny and fold, you'll never get anywhere. The trick is to get proficient at finding direction within an editor's thin reason they gave for their refusal. You may find a few scraps of information within one of the rejection letters, and decide on a rewrite.

There is an old Native American story that while slightly corny, is appropriate. A Native American Cherokee was teaching his grandchildren about life. He said to them, "A fight is going on inside me, it is a terrible fight and it is between two wolves. One wolf is evil---he is fear, anger, paranoia, envy, sorrow, regret, greed, arrogance, self-pity, guilt, resentment, inferiority, lies, false pride, competition, superiority, and ego. The other is good ---he is joy, peace, love, hope, sharing, serenity, humility, kindness, benevolence, friendship, empathy, generosity, truth, compassion and faith. This same fight is going on inside you, and inside every other person, too." They thought about it for a minute and then one child asked his grandfather, "Which wolf will win?" The old Cherokee simply replied, "The one you feed."

Life sometimes doesn't go your way. Your feelings will at some point be overruled by money and other motivations. These decisions may advance business and disappoint fifty people. One of them may be you. This is the way it works so get used to it. If every setback sends your mind into a tailspin, you'll be mired in recovery from emotional injury for the rest of your life. If you feel like giving up, go rent the movie "Rudy". You'll feel better.

"Depression is merely anger without enthusiasm"
~ Steven Wright – Comedian

18. Please everyone

In business, you *will* get into a situation where you have to make a harsh decision and upset someone, it's a matter of time. Business is business. If someone isn't doing their job, you will get pushed to a breaking point when their excuses start to pile up. Some people will be more trouble to employ than the benefit they bring to your company. Cut them from the team and move on. No explanations.

"If you want to achieve greatness stop asking for permission."
~Anonymous

19. There are no stupid questions

There are plenty of stupid questions. There are also too many questions. There is also unscrupulously pumping someone for a pile of information and not giving them any business. All of these things get on people's nerves. Whenever you contact a seasoned professional for any reason, do your homework. Find out as much as you can about the company he works for or the business he's in before you meet with him or her. You can usually do this in a few minutes on the Net. Be prepared. Keep ignorant inquiries to an absolute minimum.

> "Advice is what you ask for when you already know the answer but wish you didn't"
> ~ *Erica Jong*

20. Hate your job

I hated a job once and the job didn't care. You knew what the job was when you took it. If your job is putting washing machines in boxes, then put the stupid washing machines in the boxes. Your boss doesn't owe you a career for goodness sakes, you are simply trading your time for his money. That's it. *You only have a job because your boss thinks you care what he wants.* Do not identify yourself with your job. Your job isn't you. Do the work and smile a lot. Every other emotion is useless.

> "If hard work were such a wonderful thing, the rich would have kept it all to themselves"
> ~ *Lane Kirkland*

21. Carry a credit card balance

Running credit cards up is like digging a bigger hole every month and having the same amount of dirt to fill it. Credit card abuse is an up two down three proposition, so pay off those cards every month. Use credit cards as little as possible, and don't charge expendables like gas or dinner out. Pay cash. Charging dinner at a restaurant is stupid. Think about it: you're financing a pizza. Bad investment.

Consider how banks generate revenue. Banks always use the famous "OPM" or "other people's money" to create an income. They use your money to make money. Banks utilize a simple process called addition and subtraction. If you deposit $100, they may give you 2% interest. Then, they loan the money to someone else, charge 6% and keep the 4% difference. You need to do this for yourself.

The opposite of this formula is how most people mismanage their money. They invest in a one-year CD at 3% while carrying a car loan at 7% and credit card balances at 12%. Think about this for a minute, you're bringing in 3% on the one hand while spending 12% on the other. This is precisely why the rich get richer and the poor get poorer. What would you do if you had $5,000 in credit card debt at an 18% interest rate and were given $5,000? Would you invest in a mutual fund or pay off the credit card? Most of us would think to invest. However, the mutual fund may only pay 8%, and since the credit card may be charging you 18%, you would be in the hole 10% if you invested the money in stocks. This is the essence of negative cash flow.

You need to reverse negative cash flow. Let's look at positive cash flow using a real estate investment example. The key is: *you need to insure you can make more money with the money you borrow than the cost of the loan.* So, if a loan costs you 6%, and you can make 12% with the money, do it. Always make more money in investments than you are paying on your debt. Let's say you want to buy a house and rent it out. We'll do the simplest part of the calculation first, the basic interest cash flow, ignoring tax implications, maintenance and the appreciation of the home. We will just look at the *cost* of the loan per year compared to the *return*. Assume the house is worth $100,000 and the rental income per year is $10,000. That's a 10% return per year. If your loan payments total $4,000 per year, then your cost would be 4%. So your monthly cash flow would the difference between 10% and 4%, or 6%.

Before investing in anything, always take the total amount involved (what the house is worth in this case), and then compare cost percentage (the monthly *payment* x 12 divided by house value) to return percentage (the monthly *income* x 12 divided by house value). Then, subtract the cost percentage from the income, and you get investment return percentage. This is the essence of analyzing income investments of any kind.

You certainly need to assess risks involved in any investment, but creating cash flow is often more lucrative than creating a savings. In other words, investing in rental property and creating cash flow may be better than investing in the stock market. If you get in trouble, you can sell the property. If stocks go down, they just go down. In addition, you can borrow (leverage) a loan using the real estate as collateral. You cannot borrow money against stocks.

There is no point in doing any investing until your credit cards and other high interest loans are paid off. Positive cash flow exists when the "percentage river" is flowing towards you. Always pay off high interest debt first, and then invest. Banks somehow forget to share this information.

"Annual income twenty pounds, annual expenditure nineteen six, result happiness. "Annual income twenty pounds, annual expenditure twenty pound ought and six, result misery."
~ *Charles Dickens*

22. Borrow money from relatives

Good idea. Never again get invited to Thanksgiving. If you're stupid enough to pitch an idea to your uncle, he may reluctantly give you a loan. If by some chance your business fails and you default, you will be labeled a loser and a deadbeat for the rest of your life. If your business takes off and you do pay him back, he'll be a little miffed that you aren't sharing the spoils. Giving in to the temptation to borrow money from relatives is probably one of the worst things you can do. There are plenty of other places to secure a loan, so figure it out.

> "There are four things in the world that don't mix –
> oil and water, and money and relatives"
> ~ *Unknown*

23. Get into a partnership with a friend

I would skip this concept. Along with managing the hopes, desires and emotions of business, you get to split the profits. Plus, in the event of a business train wreck, you also have to split the debt. Starting a business is hard enough without intermingling someone else's dreams and expectations. Yes, partnerships with friends work sometimes, but they end up in the toilet more often than not.

In addition, there are far more issues to think about in a partnership situation. Partners must consider distribution of assets, duration of the partnership, assets invested by each partner, and possible division of loss in the event of failure. As you can probably imagine, partnerships can get emotionally unmanageable in a hurry, even though the parties involved had seemingly plausible intentions at the outset. Companies don't have two CEOs, and for good reason.

Managing partnership issues will invade your focus of actually running the business. As far as I'm concerned, the partnership business model should be renamed "how to lose friends and start fights".

"When two people in business together always agree,
one of them is unnecessary"
~ *Bob Goldenberg*

24. Keep lousy records

If you would like to end up in a white jacket in a padded room, keep rotten records. Keeping decent records is actually quite easy. Keep all of your receipts and invoices, and record all expenditures. Put them in manila folders. Do this every day so it doesn't pile up. Your accountant will need all of this information when tax day comes. Also, keep good records on your clients. They love it when you remember their address, and their wife's name. Information is the key in business as you move forward, and it's critical to know where you've been.

"For every minute spent in organizing, an hour is earned"
~ Benjamin Franklin

25. Be a flake

Deliver what you promise, and don't promise what you can't deliver. Solid business contacts are worth their weight in gold, literally. Shooting your mouth off with false, unsupported claims to action are deadly. One empty promise will permanently sink a good business contact. You will have a very difficult time convincing a bank you'll repay the money *this* time if they give you one more chance.

"It takes years to build up trust, and it only takes suspicion, not proof, to destroy it"
~Unknown

26. Never give up

Never give up is an insufferable mantra. It's right up there with hold on to your dreams. Barf. In order to move on with your life on any front you have to give up something else. If I move to a new house I have to give up the old one.

To take a new job I have to quit the one I have. If you have been trying to do something for years and all you have done is sucked pond water then drop it. There is a term in business called the *sunk cost fallacy*. A "sunk cost" is an expense you cannot get back. Advertising expenses or website development are good examples of "sunk costs". The sunk cost fallacy runs something like this: "I've put a lot of time and money into this so I should stay with it". This is an incorrect way to convince yourself to stay with a failure.

Big corporations entertain and thoroughly investigate many ideas before deciding on just one. You can realistically only pursue one out of ten ideas, or maybe only one out of twenty. Even big corporations don't have the resources to fully develop every idea, and neither do you.

Rather than always focusing on what to pursue, the secret to success is also driven by what businesses to avoid or discharge after a valiant attempt. Carry a notebook. Write down every idea that crosses your mind then pick the best ones later. Come up with an idea, gather some information, start the project, try not to spend too much money, then decide after six months or so weather or not it makes any sense to continue.

We all like to fawn over the stories of the actor who spent decades as a carpenter only to be discovered in his '40s and land a TV series. What usually happens is they spend their whole lives working in a restaurant and hang their hat on one national advertisement they did ten years ago. My great uncle was a drummer in a band. *On the weekends.*

During the week he was a plaster contractor building most of the houses in San Francisco. He knew that the chances of becoming a highly paid drummer was effectively zero. Most vocations that are fashionable and desirable are scarce. Hold onto your dreams? Don't give up? Don't be an idiot. If something isn't working cut your losses and move on.

What is a good batting average in baseball? 200? 250? 300? Even a 300 only lands you on first base three out of ten times. Dumping things that don't make money is part of the corporate decision making process. Corporations have the billions; so follow the behavior of the people with the cash.

> "Diversification is a hedge for ignorance"
> ~ *William O'Neil*

27. Follow your passion

Attempting to do what you love and also make money doing it narrows your chances for success down to near zero. Keep this in mind: most millionaires made their money doing something mundane. (In fact, most millionaires make their money in real estate, but that's another book.) I'm not saying don't follow your dreams, but don't excuse an opportunity to make money simply because the opportunity isn't glamorous. If you start selling something boring that makes big money all of a sudden it becomes very interesting.

Don't look at business concepts emotionally or fondly. Look at business the way big business looks at it: does it turn a hefty profit or doesn't it? You may not realize it yet, but you want success, freedom and independence. You want the power to make decisions on your own terms. You do not care about tennis rackets or car parts.

This brings me to an argument that rages between children and parents in every household every day in every country on the planet. The argument grows from a basic misunderstanding that there are *two distinct career types*. The two types of careers are: the "practical" career, and the "fantasy" career.

a) Practical careers are: Doctor, lawyer, marketing executive, programmer, graphic artist, civil engineer, chemist, business administrator, etc. These are the kinds of careers that are readily available and make sense, so parents and schools like them.
b) Fantasy careers are: fighter pilot, movie star, rock star, children's book author, and so on. The problem is, the cull ratio for the fantasy careers is outrageously high, simply because everyone wants to be a racecar driver or a movie star.

Deciding on a single income or pursuing a single glittering career in this world is an unbelievably dumb thing to do. Spending the rest of your life expecting to combine cash flow and charm is totally juvenile. Please don't even try and tell me you would excuse a million dollar a year shoelace business because you would rather be a country western singer. Go for two careers, maybe three. Pursue two practical careers and one fantasy career. Get a degree in something marketable, get your contractor's license and write a children's book. The degree and the contractor's license have a high probability for success. However, as fun as the children's book is to write, the chances for monetary success in the children's book market is basically nil.

The common scholastic sales pitch for success is to combine making money *and* doing what you love. This is an attempt to merge two things that are very difficult to achieve even on their own. Fine. Go get two baseballs and a felt pen. Write "money" on one baseball and "fantasy career" on the other. Now throw them in the air, close your eyes and try to catch both balls. Good luck.

There is one CEO and thousands of employees. There is one successful actor and tens of thousands of waiters who claim to be actors. Be open to anything that makes money, including the pedestrian. Accept any opportunity to make money even if it makes for a boring conversation at a party.

"When it comes to cash, if enough is good, more is better and too much is just right"
~ Larry Jennings – Philosopher

28. Be all you can be

More unattainable scholastic rhetorical vomit. Try to be *part* of what you can be. I generally go for between 65-70% of what I can be. That's pretty high, really. Our society is way too hung up on excellence. We get wrapped up in the number one this and top that. Pay attention to the ramblings in the news. The three top billionaires are always in the forefront of the mind of our collective consciousness. What about the fifty seventh richest man? Does he have an opinion? I'll bet he's loaded. Give yourself a bunch of credit as you claw your way to the middle. I have seen people actually decline to buy a lottery ticket because the jackpot was only nine million. What? Does it always have to be some foolish amount before anyone is interested? If I dropped a quarter of a million in your lap your life would be different immediately. Set goals, but be reasonable. Attainable goals are much more satisfying to achieve than incessantly expecting the outrageous.

"Expectation is the mother of all frustration"
~ *Antonio Banderas*

Section 3
Hate the Corporation

29. It's lonely at the top

It's lonely at the top like it's disappointing to win a race. This comment is right up there with "money doesn't buy happiness". I guess this means there are hundreds of executive vice presidents who would turn down a promotion to run a corporation because it would be lonely and no fun. Bother yourself to get to the top of your game. You won't be lonely for cash, and you get to enjoy the view.

> "You have reached the pinnacle of success as
> soon as you become uninterested in money,
> compliments, or publicity"
> ~ *Thomas Wolfe*

30. Mix business relationships

Never mix business relationships. If you make gift baskets or jewelry and your contractor comes over to fix the sink, DO NOT try to sell him a gift basket or a bracelet.
This practice always backfires. A similar social disaster is created with these home business parties where you stumble through desperately trying to sell your friends spatulas or sustainable chocolate bars from some appealing far flung country. If you are paying someone for something, don't try to rope them into buying something from you.

Always awkward.

> "Mixing business with personal matters always leads to damaged relationships, and poor business decisions."
> ~ *Anonymous*

31. Get bound by time

I am going to take credit for making this term up, because I did. There are many business models and structures. I feel that there are, above all, two categories: *time bound* and *non-time bound*. The acid test for any business venture involves the concept of what I call *time binding*. Here is how this works. I am going to open a yoga studio. I can book four classes a day, and each class has ten students, that's forty students per day. If I charge ten dollars each, that's four hundred dollars. That's it. I can't pack twice as many classes in the same studio, nor can I double book the class number.

I may be boxed in by room size or possibly fire regulations. Therefore, a yoga studio business model is by definition "bound by time". So then is a cobbler, a plumber, or an auto repair shop. These would all define the concept of a time bound business.

The opposite would be a non-time bound business. Let's say you design an app for cell phones. You design the app and get it posted on Google play. You sell one copy. Then ten. Then a hundred. Did you have to make more? No. Did you have to rent more space? No. You could sell a thousand or ten thousand a day and do no more work. This business model is a non-bound by time business.

Think about the big corporations, I'm referring to the ones that own the skyscrapers. Very few of them are time bound businesses. They all charge based on use, or get a percentage of the action. Non time bound businesses are things like phone companies, insurance companies, and software manufacturers.

If you want to open a Karate studio and you're really hung up on it, knock yourself out, but a Karate studio is on no uncertain terms the definition of a time bound business.

"The future isn't what it used to be"
~ *Yogi Berra*

32. Be a team player

I love being told to be a team player, since I really like being insulted. It's always some stiff making six figures who is informing me I need to be a "team player". I'm quite sure that when they receive a hefty bonus they're in no hurry to share it with their "team". Let's get serious. If you're working for someone else you're playing on the "shut up and follow orders" team.

No president or CEO ever got to the top through "proper channels". Managers who expect you to say on track, their track, have manufactured every rule in the world. What about your rules? I'm not telling you to lie cheat or steal, these things always come back and bite you. However, attempting to get rich by walking through the front door is foolishness, and will leave you sucking pond water through the same microscopic straw that everyone else is.

"Any fool can make a rule, and any fool will mind it"
~ Henry David Thoreau

33. My company can't get by without me

Your company can get by without you like a swimming pool can get by without a cup of water. "I don't know if my company can get by without me" is a thin, narcissistic stupid fantasy we like to invent to create importance from nothing. The fact is, as an employee, you're a problem. You're an expense. I'm sure you've noticed that corporations get rid of employees to boost profits. In fact, you need to produce ten times the amount of money your company gives you for your job to be justified. This is why corporations keep marketing executives and fire janitors when they need to make cuts. The marketing people produce income; the janitorial staff is unfortunately an expense. It sucks, but it's true.

"All paid jobs absorb and degrade the mind"
~ *Aristotle (384BC – 322BC)*

34. Do your own accounting

The first thing you need to know about accounting is: *hire an accountant*. You're not going to save a dime screwing around trying to do your own books. Don't think for a minute that you can deal with the complexities of business taxes and cash flow on your own. You have too much other stuff to do.

When it comes to "the books" there are two documents you need to understand. The first is called the *Profit and Loss* statement, or the "P and L". This document essentially flows from top to bottom, and compares, or subtracts *income* from *expenses* leaving you with *profit*. At the top of the P&L is your gross *income*. Below that, are your *expenses*. At the bottom is your *net profit*. Then there are of course the taxes. If you compare an individual P&L and a business P&L, you will notice one glaring difference. The difference is the *positioning* of the taxes. For an individual, taxes are listed *before* expenses. For a business, they come *after* expenses. Therefore, in a business you get to deduct your expenses and reduce your gross income by the amount you spent to run the business. As an individual, you don't.

The profit and loss statement is where the famous "bottom line" phrase comes from. The bottom line is your net profit after expenses and taxes. Whatever doesn't leave your grasp after gross income is profit.

There is one more line on a P&L that comes into play if you run a business that sells products or durable goods. This line is called "Cost of goods sold". This simply refers to the purchase cost of the product before a sale is made. In other words, *how much the inventory costs to buy*. When you "buy" inventory, you really aren't spending the money. You are converting the money from a liquid asset, or cash, into an inventory asset. You technically still have the money. The cost of the product only becomes an expense the moment the product is sold. The "cost of goods sold" line item is deducted *after* gross income but *before* expenses.

The second document you need to concern yourself with is called a *Balance Sheet*. This document is arranged side by side. The balance sheet compares *assets* to *liabilities*. An *asset* would be the equity (what part you own) on your house, how much you have in the bank, how much your car is worth if it's paid for, etc. Your *liabilities* are how much you *owe* on your house, how much you *owe* on your credit cards, etc. Here comes the balance part. If you sold your house and your car, emptied your bank account, then paid all of your bills, mortgage, car loan etc., would you have any money left over or would you be in the hole?

These documents are easy to try out. Make up a P&L next month. Keep all of your receipts and paychecks for the month. List your income at the top, deduct all of your expenses, and then calculate your subsequent net profit for the month. Then make up a balance sheet. List all of your assets, money in the bank, how much your car is worth, how much your house is worth, etc. Then calculate your liabilities. What you owe on your house, how much you owe on your car, credit cards, etc. Then, subtract what you owe from what you own. There's your P&L and your balance sheet.

Ignoring these two documents is the road to bankruptcy. *Bankruptcy is when you owe far more than you own, and your income will no longer cover fixed expenses combined with the payments on your liability.* Gosh, that was fun. Now go get a phone book and find an accountant.

"A budget is simply a mathematical
confirmation of your suspicions"
~ *A.A. Latimer*

35. Walk into a negotiation with no options

This is akin to walking into your boss's office and asking for a raise based on the fact that you're a nice guy. Volumes of books have been written on this subject, and most are wrong. Often, people speak of how to "ask" for a raise. This is incorrect. You are not asking, you're telling your employer how much money you are going to be making or you're going to quit. You do not need to be nasty or demanding, because negotiating is a compromise.

Remember: your boss doesn't ever want to give you any more money. Companies have always had a bad quarter and can't afford anything. Therefore, it needs to be more of a problem for him to find someone to replace you than it will cost him to give you a raise. The secret is, you need to own the ability to walk out, and you must be prepared to do it. If you "need" the job when negotiating a raise, that fact will come out of your pores and you will get nothing. Need is a four letter word. If you "need", you're screwed. Getting a raise requires options. The first option you will need is a job offer if you mess this up.

A terrific negotiating tool in any situation is the "two option" method. If you are negotiating for a new car, don't get into a push pull wherein you have one price in mind and the salesperson has another. Remember, car salesmen are professional negotiators. *When you are in a negotiation, always give the other person two options, then sit and relax.* Start by saying, "look, this can go two ways, you either give me the lower price, or I'll pay the higher price and you give me the extended warranty and the undercoating".

Make sure you will be satisfied with either option, *since you are going to force the other person to pick one.* If he tries to say, "we'll give you the undercoating but not the extended warranty", you reply, "that was not one of the two options". Then sit and be quiet. You have the money, so you always have the option of walking out.

Walking into any negotiation with no options is like playing poker with one card. In any negotiating situation, gently let the other person know what you feel is fair, without showing your hand. In other words, you up the bet, and don't let them know you'll walk if they refuse.

"The greatest power in the world is the power to say no"
~ Katharine Hepburn

36. The customer is always right

The customer is not always right. Some customers are a pain in the you-know-what. Some screwy customers seem to take great issue with the fact that you have made a profit and will grind your company on a washboard until they get their money back. In any business, keep a blacklist. A successful business will depend on the customers you select, as well as the ones you don't. When giving an estimate, a contractor is interviewing the client as much as the client is interviewing the contractor.

"Never underestimate the power of an irate customer"
~ *Joel E. Ross*

Section 4
You and business narcissism

"... I believe I've gotten myself into sufficient debt to qualify for the American dream..."

37. "I" want to start "my" own business

Here's a newsflash: nobody cares about you, or what you want. Other people care about themselves and what they want, and that's the end of it. If you hear of someone else who found a bag of money, you're expected to be happy for them and their good fortune. Sure, for about three seconds. Then you get a little down on your own life and you dream of what you could have done with the cash. We outwardly care about others, but internally think of ourselves. So, when considering any business, always view the business with other people's selfishness in mind.

Let's rewrite that common phrase "I want to start my own business". It really should read something like, "I'm going to find out what people want, and then I'm going to provide them with it". That's much more accurate. "I want to open a Cuban restaurant", should be phrased, "I need to research how many people in the area are interested in Cuban food, and if there is any competition for that type of cuisine".

Don't decide on what to sell by deciding what you want to sell. Don't make business decisions based on your personal taste. When considering any business venture, always approach from what feels like the back. If you're going to open an expensive restaurant, check with the local chamber of commerce and get the demographics to see how many rich people are in the area. If you're going to start a towing company, check with the local emergency services to see if they have sufficient call for tow trucks. Find a need and fill it, don't do something just because you've always wanted to do it.

"Customers buy for their reasons, not yours"
~ *Orvel Ray Wilson*

38. Sell products and services you like

Pay attention, here is the absolute be all end all numero-uno marketing concept: *you are not selling products or services you are selling feelings.* It makes no difference what you are selling or providing, you are selling *perceived benefits* to the customer. Drive by any open garage in the U.S. and most of them are filled to capacity with junk. These people didn't buy most of this crap because they needed it; they bought it because they thought it would improve their life. Whenever you conceive of any sales pitch or advertisement, tell the viewer they will be smarter, thinner, funnier, better looking and have more friends when they buy the product.

Consider the angle of any advertising slogan. A sports shoe advertisement doesn't exclaim how well the shoes are made or how long the company has been in business, they tell you that you will be a better basketball player. This isn't to say that "Serving the community since 1972" isn't a good point, but it's secondary. First, *sell the benefit to the customer.* Telephone companies often pitch "be closer to the ones you love". They're not selling a service; they're selling family unity. They're not selling products; they're selling feelings.

Once you have selected a business, *find out how people want to feel in that genre of business sell that feeling to them.* Put this book down. Go turn on the television and watch the ads or browse a magazine with this concept in mind. You will see that feelings are the essence of advertising.

"In the factory we make cosmetics,
in the drugstore we sell hope"
~ *Charles Revson*

39. Sell cheap junk

Hey! I can get a whole bunch of $2 glow in the dark shoelaces and sell them on e-bay! Don't be an idiot. Selling cheap stuff is much more work than selling expensive stuff. Selling cheap junk creates an unnecessarily lopsided "effort to return" ratio. It takes just as long to run a credit card for $43 as it does to run it for $453, and it takes just as much time to box up a cheap item as it does an expensive one. Therefore: to make the same money, it is exactly twice as much work to sell a $1 item as it is to sell a $2 item. Let's compare selling a $50 item to a $250 item. If I sell 50 $250 items, that's $12,500 in gross sales. To make that same amount selling $50 items, I have to sell 250 items, or five times the sales volume. Not to mention five times the postage, five times the boxes, and five times the trouble.

The lopsided "effort to return" axiom also applies to advertising. First, consider the god of advertising, which is called the *conversion rate*. The conversion rate refers to the number of copies of an advertisement that are distributed, divided by the number of responses you get. Therefore, if 100 copies of a magazine are sold and one person calls, the response conversion rate is 1%.

It may not seem like an obvious parallel to draw, but there is a powerful link between the *price of the product* and the *advertising conversion rate*. The cheaper the product, the more effective your advertising has to be. Conversely, the more expensive the product, the less effective your advertisement needs to be. Let's say you sell a product that retails for $100, and the profit is $50. If you run a $500 ad, you will have to sell ten of these items to break even on the ad (ten sales conversions). However, if you sell a $500 product and you run a $500 ad, you will only have to sell two of your products to break even on the cost of the advertisement (only two sales conversions).

Therefore, eighty percent more people will have to buy your item to make the ad work in the case of the less expensive product. Therefore, when the price of the item goes up, your expenses and effort go down.

Don't worry about the prices of various products based on notions of money. People will pay $30,000 for a new car they really don't need, then complain that gas went up 10¢ a gallon. Everything is relative, and everything is a perception. Carry what people buy and charge what they will pay. Sell the most expensive product you can sell.

> "There was a time when a fool and his money were soon parted, but now it happens to everybody"
> ~ *Adlai Stevenson*

40. Offer services nobody wants to pay for

There are certain vocations that customers strangely expect to be free. People don't mind paying for cars, houses, and groceries. Even certain kinds of labor have accepted costs such as construction, automobile repairs, etc. However, services like interior design, graphic design, and more recently web design often carry a perception of being easy to do, so people expect them to be inexpensive.

I realize there could be an argument made that there are many successful web and interior designers. However, most interior designers make a large portion of their income bringing clients to wholesale furniture stores (where the designers receive deep discounts), then sell the furniture to the clients at retail. This way, their design fee can remain what seems to be reasonable, and the real profits are hidden in the furniture. The customers just don't see it. A customer wouldn't make much of a fuss paying $4,000 for custom furniture and a $500 design fee; however, they would cry a river if the furniture was $2,000 and the design fee was $2,500. It really doesn't matter where you make the money; the customer just needs to agree with you.

"Everything is worth what the purchaser will pay for it"
~ *Publilius Syrus (100 BC)*

41. Build a dam and hope for rain

This is the biggest mistake most first time business owners make: they set the business up first. You may rent a building, find suppliers, buy stock then secure a phone number and a credit card machine. This is in fact the easy part, and it's backwards. Before you do anything, you need to test the concept and see if anyone notices. Let's say you want to start a gift basket company. Rather than finding suppliers for soap, baskets, filler, and maybe opening a store, do a marketing test first. Get the bad news over with.

Find a gift basket company in another town and buy ten gift baskets. Then, go to five grocery stores in *your* town and find the buyer. Give them the gift baskets (yes, give) and say, "I'm starting a gift basket company and I would like to give you these samples. Please put these in your store and call me when they sell, you can keep all of the money". I know this sound strange, but you need to grease the storeowner with some free stuff to get vital information. Sit and wait for the phone to ring. Log every call from each store, and the day the basket sold. Then you can add up how fast they sold, and what your profit margin would be if you had supplied them yourself. A twist on this concept would be to supply the stores with gift baskets, but at different prices. This way, you will not only find out if anybody wants gift baskets, but what price sells the fastest. You would then calculate the cost to manufacture the product in reverse. If the basket priced at $54 sold the fastest, that means your cost per basket can be only $27 in order to make a profit.

By doing a marketing test first, you can calculate how many stores your baskets will need to be in to make the business worth doing. You complete the test by adding up how many baskets sold and divide it into how much you want to make a year. If you sell two baskets per week per store, multiply the total income per store by 52 (weeks in the year) and divide it into what you want for gross profit. Then you will know how many stores you will need to be in to make it happen. I guarantee this little mathematics exercise will take less time and be less expensive than setting up the business first and finding out nobody wants gift baskets. Hence: make sure there's water in the river before you build the dam.

> "First get your facts;
> then you can distort them at your leisure"
> *~ Mark Twain*

42. Throw money at a business to get it to happen

It takes money to make money is not always true. Many businesses certainly require setup costs, but many do not. If you are going to to open a restaurant you will likely need a half a million dollars you're not real fond of to get going. Building leases, refrigerators, stoves, chairs, tables, health inspections, etc. There are plenty of ventures one can embark upon that have a very low, and sometimes non-existent startup cost. I have more than a few examples of friends and or acquaintances who have dumped six figures into a business and had it go south in a month. One coffee shop comes to mind. The startup cost for this experiment was north of $100K (money borrowed from a friend, by the way - don't get me started) all of which was spent and lost in a few months. This particular person who lost the coffee shop lost the friend, too.

Consider the coffee shop. How about a coffee kiosk? One of those things whith the wheels on it. Startup on that would be in the hundreds, or maybe thousands, not hundreds of thousands. Yes, start a business. But learn the ins outs of a business for as little money up front as possible. Do yourself a favor and avoid thinking that if you spend a bunch of money opening a store that fact alone will get people to care.

"Waste neither time nor money, but make the best use of both"
~ Benjamin Franklin

Section 5
Yak it up to the wrong people

"It's not that I don't like your idea,
I just don't want you to fail miserably"

43. Incessantly share with others

Even though you're probably feeling like a puppy in a box at the supermarket, do not under any circumstances give in to the temptation to yap details of your intentions to passersby, people you are sitting next to on the plane, relatives, or anyone not directly connected to your endeavor. What are you, five? If you come up with a good idea, don't talk about it, do it. There is an appropriate World War II slogan that states, "loose lips sink ships". Talking too much *always* steals your energy. The more people you share your ideas with, the less your ideas belong to you. *What you are really looking for by sharing intentions with friends or relatives is approval and a reassuring pat on the back.* I hate to be a pessimist, but you probably won't get it. Therefore, don't let the purity of your concept become infected with other people's opinions.

Indiscriminate information volunteering always places an "expectation marker". Everyone you share your plans with will expect detailed progress updates based on *their* expectations next time they see you. Avoid this. Don't even tell people you're not telling them anything. The general population will often insist that withholding information is being dishonest. Not true. Dishonesty is the act of purposefully offering incorrect information. Not saying anything is just not saying anything.

Running a business has the distinction of being one of the only activities that a chosen few ever attempt, and yet everyone has an opinion on how it should be done. If you would like to learn how to ride a horse, you would never ask someone who did not ride horses what you should do. Running a business is no different.

The best way to handle a small business oriented conversation at a party, (even if the person you're speaking to is also starting their own endeavor and you feel as if you may have something in common), is to ask the other person questions about what *they* are doing. The fact of the matter is, everybody in the free world has, "a great idea" and "is working a deal with someone". Ignore your urge to share and focus on staying in control of the conversation. Stay in control of the situation by innocently asking veiled questions such as, "How are you going to advertise?" or, "have you landed any customers?" At this point, they will most probably start revealing enough specific details about their intentions to fill the Library of Congress. Listen to their intentions, listen to things they have tried, and listen to their plans. Nine times out of ten you'll find that most people's ideas are just that, ideas. When you are done listening, and you need to refill your punch glass, wish them the best of luck and walk away. *You will obtain volumes of information by listening and gain nothing by talking.*

The rest of the people on this planet will rarely analyze your fantastic ideas at face value. They will criticize or want to help. This is *never* what you had in mind. The person you are speaking to has an opinion of you. They may think you're a go-getter, a dreamer, or a liar. Therefore, people will analyze your idea based on this predisposed opinion. If they don't see you as a famous writer, your intention to become a writer will be questioned not based on your ability, but based on the fact that they see you as a mechanic. Don't tell anyone anything unless you are prepared to accept or deflect an opinion.

Therefore, do not share your ideas with people who might be threatened by your success, or who might be left behind. Only share your ideas with others who are active doers themselves. Essentially, if a person is not comfortable with their own accomplishments, they certainly aren't going to be comfortable with yours. *Only seek advice from an experienced, neutral third party.* To fully understand another person's support or resistance to your idea, you must take one giant step backward and analyze their motivation. Is this person going to benefit or be hurt by my success?

Burt Rutan is an innovative aircraft designer. His designs are largely atypical, asymmetrical, and uncommon. One of his more notable designs was the Voyager, which was the first aircraft to make it around the world on one tank of fuel. More recently, he designed "SpaceShipOne", the first privately funded craft to make it into space. He is a man who constantly explores new territories in aviation. Burt Rutan has a strict rule. He never discusses his current projects until the designs have flown. He avoids prying eyes, pointed questions and unsolicited opinions. He especially doesn't have to justify intentions and design choices, and he can start and stop projects without offering explanation. This is his policy and it should also be yours.

"He who knows does not speak…
he who speaks does not know"
~ Lao-Tzu - Chinese philosopher (604-531BC)

44. Hang out with losers

This is always a big help. Unsuccessful, unmotivated people are not only uncooperative while you navigate through a life change, they will probably attempt to hold you back. Since they're not doing anything with their life, they will totally resent your quest for success. Keep in mind that every new idea that changed the world was hard fought. Everyone thought Columbus was crazy, and most ridiculed Robert Goddard, the inventor of the modern rocket, during his extensive tests. The fact of the matter is; successful people hang out with successful people.

Another way to look at loser relationships is in the mirror, your mirror. At the risk of sounding like a therapist, you may have chosen a loser friend as a result of how you feel about yourself. If you have low self-esteem, you will most likely select friends who reinforce how you feel. People with a rotten self-image usually pick friends who put them down and hold them back. *You may be selecting friends who actually help you maintain failure.* This is the epitome of the self-fulfilling prophecy, "I feel like crap about myself and this jerk won't leave me alone". As soon as you decide to feel better, you will drop your interest in the loser. When he or she calls, you'll be busy.

> "Great spirits have always encountered violent opposition from mediocre minds"
> ~ *Albert Einstein*

45. Toil endlessly with another person's "Venue"

Venue is the portion of a mind that controls the background substance of any discussion. A person's "venue" can be described as their shtick or comfort zone. Venue is how far off center a listener is going to let you get before they cry foul, governed by their view of life. Is their glass half full or half empty? If the person you are talking to thinks that their life stinks, then your idea will stink as far as they are concerned. There is nowhere else for them to go.

You also have a venue. Think of what it is. It may be holding you back. It may be a lack of perceived worthiness, absurd expectations, or entrenched lifelong issues. Getting rid of your own negative venue is a giant step towards success.

Psychological venue lies behind every issue, and behind any subject. The perceived potential of any concept is governed only by the boundaries of the minds involved. As you interact with another person, pay attention to the emotional limitations behind the rhetoric. If you listen carefully, you will find the limits of their soul.

"The Smaller the mind the greater the conceit"
~ Aesop
Greek slave & fable author (620 BC - 560 BC)

46. Hang out with evil, condescending control freaks

There are two kinds of people in this world: people who build you up, and people who tear you down. You will notice that people who build you up are the people you aspire to be like. It sometimes helps to actually ask the question: do I want to be like this person? Do I want this person to represent a part of my life? Oddly enough, even though we do not admire or want to be like people who tear us down, we for some reason feel compelled to appease these creatures with our hopes and dreams in a vain attempt to make a point.

When you are caught in the undertow of a control freak, you will find yourself nowhere else but perpetually mired in limbo constantly explaining yourself and apologizing for your behavior. You will never be permitted to explain yourself, *because the fact that you can't explain yourself is the essence of the game*. Controlling other people is the control freak's "venue". In the company of a control freak, you will never get anything done. In the company of a person who honestly wants you to succeed, things start to happen.

The fundamental difference between a honest to goodness supportive person and a control freak is as follows: the supportive person will hear your ideas and aspirations and *actually do something like pick up the phone or take you to meet an important contact.* A control freak on the other hand will *say* they're supportive, but actively stop any attempt at forward motion. When the rubber actually hits the road, the supportive person will *take action to assist your progress*, and the control freak *will do everything he can to stop you.*

These are the five warning signs that you are in the vicinity of an evil control freak:

1) They will tell you they like you. They will claim the world is your oyster, and you possess vast stores of untapped talent. However, they're disappointed that you're not using it. It makes them sad that you're a slacker.
2) If you ever try to implement the "vast stores of talent" they declare you possess, every idea you come up with will be smoothly shot down. Your ideas will be torn to pieces through examples of others who have tried and failed. They will strip the energy from every concept you present to help you avoid humiliating failure.
3) They will jokingly put you down in front of other people. If you pull them aside later and protest their putdown, they will claim they were "just kidding" and *you* are over reacting.
4) They will expect you to accept every invitation they extend, but they will gracefully reject all of yours. These people will also point out that *their* friends have won a triathlon and golf with the President. They will subsequently criticize *your* choice of friends.
5) If you do have a falling out with one of these people, they will become sticky sweet, and will attempt to reestablish contact through the use of gifts or by having one of their friends call you and inquire what *your* problem is. They never apologize of course, you do.

Control freaks employ an ancient method of arguing to maintain their control. These people make use of a fascinating three thousand year old Latin legal term. This type of putdown is a Latin logical fallacy called "Argumentum ad Hominem", or "argument to the man".

The ad hominem fallacy transforms an assertion on a given topic made by person "A" into a personal attack by person "B" directed back at person "A". It works like this: if you say, "the computer is acting up" the ad hominem response would be, "what are you, the new computer expert?" This putdown literally involves redirecting the conversation from the original topic to an assault directed *at you*. The ad hominem argument alleges that you do not have the knowledge or experience to make a valid statement. If a father says to a child, "pick up your toys", the child's ad hominem response would be, "you're mean". The child has now redirected the discussion from the mess of toys, which is the topic, to the disposition of the parent. The parent is now the one with the problem. Herein begins the fight.

Ad hominem arguments start wars and end marriages. Now you know what it is, if anyone tries to pull an ad hominem redirect, you have my permission to tie their shoelaces together, or at least tell them to stay on the subject.

Control freak manipulators use another tactic that is highly effective. I call it the "manipulation triangle". Manipulators create this triangle by "cutting out" a weak person to push around, but reserving an audience of people and friends who are always treated very well. This way, the manipulated person feels singled out - because they are. The old, "if he does it to you he does it to everyone" assertion is not true. The manipulator cannot attempt to manipulate everyone, because then the entire group would label him or her a jerk.

The three players in the manipulation triangle are:
1) The manipulator – This is the person who sets the stage. This person controls the manipulated and the audience.
2) The manipulated – This person is trapped, pushed around, and put off, then subsequently blamed for the incident after the game runs its course. The manipulated always comes up short.
3) The audience – These players exist to support the manipulator. The audience is unaware that they are involved. They are pre-positioned by the manipulator to be under the impression they are mediating. In fact, the manipulator has installed the audience to reinforce the manipulator's case. When the manipulated arrives looking for support, the audience tells the poor fool to calm down and be reasonable.

These three factions come together in many venues. The simplest example would be the proverbial younger child who breaks the lamp. The older child rats out the younger child to the mother, expecting praise, and the younger child throws a fit and cries. The mother subsequently scolds the older child for being a ratfink. The younger child receives comfort from the mother because the child's feelings are seen as more important than the broken lamp. The older child is the loser. Naturally, if the older child had broken the lamp, he would have been grounded for a week. The younger child is the manipulator, the older child is the manipulated, and the mother is the audience. The lamp has nothing to do with it.

The only way to stop being manipulated is to cease participating. A yes or no answer to any question posed by a manipulator starts another session of manipulation. If you say "yes" to a manipulator's request, you will be expected to perform. If you say no, you will be labeled difficult and the "no" answer will start an argument. Do not answer questions.

"Passive resistance" works well. Rather than "yes" or "no" try, "I'll get back to you" or "let me check with my wife first". You of course do not get back to them or check with your wife.

Control freaks are master manipulators. This is their forte. Going head to head with one of these people is like trying to win a tennis match against Andre Agassi. Anger and frustration aside, these people are good at what they do. Some people like to be control freaks, and some people like to play the trumpet. It's kind of the way it is. The only way to achieve nirvana and avoid torrid conversations is to limit or stop all transmission of personal information to a controller. Do not tell them what stocks you have invested in, or what car you have bought. The control freak will inform you that you've made a grievous error, no matter what you've done. Only speak to manipulators about sports or the weather. Then you can go to Hawaii and have a cream soda with a smile.

If you find yourself involved with, or in proximity to a person who fits the description of a control freak there is only one thing to do. Walk away. You can't fix it. Control freak friendship dynamics don't change, and weird family dynamics don't change. Don't bother with psychologists, psychiatrists or family therapy. You can't get anyone to see the light. Control freaks are people who are either threatened by you or don't like you. Since you cannot change these people don't bother trying.

"Associate yourself with men of quality if you esteem your
own reputation, for 'tis better to be alone
than in bad company"
~ *George Washington*

47. Tell everyone about your current lawsuit

Never talk about legal problems. If you tell people about a lawsuit you're involved in, they will perceive you as a litigious person and may not want to do business with you. First of all, avoid lawsuits at all costs. Don't let your ego get in the way of your sensibilities.

> "Avoid lawsuits beyond all things; they pervert your conscience, impair your health, and dissipate your property"
> ~ *Jean De La Bruyere*

48. Answer questions and explain yourself

Answering questions and explaining yourself is a sure fire way to get yourself in trouble. Remember: *the person who is asking the questions is always in charge of the conversation.* Think about a courtroom or a police interrogation. In both cases, the lawyer or the police officer are the people asking the questions. In fact, if a witness on the stand asks a question, the judge will instruct them to *answer questions only*. The same applies in the case of the police interrogation. The police ask the questions. This keeps the ball entirely in their court.

You can practice your "not answering questions" technique at your local electronics store when they ask you for your name and address. You do not want to give them your name and address, and they know this. That is why they have a stable of cleverly scripted questions and statements (lies) that will coerce you into spilling your personal information. When the salesperson asks, "may I have your name and address?" you calmly reply, "may I buy this item without giving you any personal information?" First of all, you did not answer their question (this is good), and the question was converted into a simple yes or no inquiry that could only be answered one way, your way.

Had you answered the sales person by saying, "I don't want to give you my personal information" this answer would have prompted the salesperson to say, "this is just for our records, we won't send out a catalog". This is of course a lie, but you permitted him to play this card by answering the question. Above all else, stay calm. Getting upset always loses ground.

The "don't explain and don't answer questions" policy is a learned skill. Practice doing this and you'll see the results. Pay attention to other people's conversations. The person asking the questions is running the show, and the person answering is always struggling to keep up.

"You can't truthfully explain your smallest action without fully revealing your character"
~ *Unknown*

49. Attempt to prove your worthiness

Friendship and family dynamics are set in stone within seconds of inception. People set boundaries for you that *they are comfortable with. Do not attempt to convince another person that it is all right to step outside the boundaries they have set for you.* You will be forever stalled in a futile struggle to convince someone that you are successful, happy, or clever. If a particular person sees you as a disappointment, it will disappoint them if you are successful.

If you're one of three sons and your Father thinks you're the goofball, then that's it. The chances you could build a spaceship, show it to your Dad and have him actually accept the accomplishment is basically nil. In your father's eyes, you are not attempting to prove your worthiness with a spaceship; you are attempting to prove his perception of you is wrong. You cannot tell people they are wrong. It makes them nervous.

"Human kind cannot bear much reality"
~ *T.S. Elliot*

50. Blab to people at work

Do not under any circumstances tell anyone at your current job that you are "starting your own business". This isn't to say that you don't work with some perfectly nice individuals, but let's get serious; these are precisely the people you are trying to get away from.

If you make the mistake of spilling the beans at work, two irreversible things will happen. First, the news that someone in the office is constructing a way out of the nine to five will spread like wildfire. This particular type of exposure is unlike mentioning your business venture to someone at a party or at a family function, which may only occur once every six months. Mentioning your idea to people you work with will bring prying questions at the coffee machine five miserable days a week.

In addition, if you are dumb enough to let the cat out of the bag at the office, that "guy at work" will offer his unsolicited opinions, and may expect to be included. Since you are not planning on taking any of these people with you when your business is booming and you jump ship, they don't need to know anything of your intentions.

The second irreversible thing that will happen if you tell someone at work is the news will ramble over to the boss' office. You will instantly lose all credibility with your superior. He will feel that your energy is focused elsewhere, and he'll be right. You would never tell the boss that you were out looking for another job, so don't tell him or anyone else at work about your idea. Businesses take more time than you think to get off the ground, so as you build your new business, you may still want the option of being considered for promotions or raises. If the brass catches wind that you've decided to start off on your own seeking riches elsewhere, you can forget being considered for advancement. Why would they promote someone who has one foot out the door?

In addition, businesses must sometimes conduct a round of layoffs. As much as we may not like to admit it, laying employees off is a difficult decision for any manager or CEO, so don't feed them the justification. Let's imagine for a moment that you're the boss and you're faced with laying people off. If you're aware that two or three of your employees have what you consider to be another valid source of income, this will greatly increase their chances of getting the ax.

This brings me to a true story recalled from years ago. A friend worked with a quiet man at a local hardware store. The quiet man initially worked on the sales floor, received raises, and was ultimately promoted to the head of the paint and wallpaper department. One Friday afternoon at 4:55 pm, he unexpectedly walked into the boss' office and gave his notice. This wasn't the traditional two weeks, as he abruptly stated that this particular Friday was his last day. The office personnel had no idea this was coming.

The following Monday morning, the same quiet man opened the doors to his new paint store *across the street* from the hardware store. The planning for this move had taken a year or more, and had he been foolish enough to leak his intentions to the management and co-workers, he would have received no raises or promotions, and would have been besieged with constant questions. Furthermore, the management wouldn't have let him anywhere near the books or their suppliers. They also wouldn't have been too pleased with the prospect of him opening a competing store within three hundred yards of their location. Not to mention he most certainly would have been fired. This in a nutshell is the lesson. Keep a lid on it at work. Not a word. I mean it.

"It's so simple to be wise.
Just think of something stupid to say and then don't say it"
~ *Sam Levenson*

51. Share your mistakes

Don't share your mistakes with people. Success and riches are commonly perceived as a *thing*, when in fact it is a *process,* and that process involves mistakes. Successful people who appear on radio and television are often introduced onscreen as having "hit it big". This state of existence suggests visuals similar to a Las Vegas jackpot, or a chance discovery of oil. Through the magic of creative television editing, this common misperception of success has been reduced to the instant it happens. The ten previous years of frustration and ice-cold rejection are conveyed as an admirable badge of courage.

You as a budding business owner will hear that other business owner's long journey to the apex of success was hard fought, and their failures were instrumental in shaping their sterling character. However, if you are stupid enough to tell someone of your failures, you will be informed that any bonehead should have known better. If you make a mistake, keep it to yourself and move on.

"Success is the ability to go from one failure to another with no loss of enthusiasm"
~ *Sir Winston Churchill*

52. Tell everyone you're an expert

Nobody wants to hear how terrific you are, they prefer to notice on their own. Volunteered information is always suspect, information that is asked for is deemed reliable.

Have you ever been talking to someone who, even though you don't ask, begins telling your what a great tennis player they are? You could care less, and you doubt the validity of what they are saying. However, if you actually witness this person playing tennis and you notice how good they are, you're much more likely to be impressed. Big difference. So don't tell people how terrific you are, wait until they notice.

There's another problem with getting chatty about your virtues. If you're pompous enough to tell everyone you're a computer expert, your services will soon be expected. "Hey, can you take a look at my computer?", they'll say, anticipating immediate results. You'll fiddle and prod, ultimately destroying your afternoon and most likely your co-worker's computer. Even if you are lucky enough to fix it, you are now his personal computer consultant. The next time something bad happens to his computer, it will be your fault. Your phone will ring at 11:30 p.m., and you'll be expected to drive over there and deal with it.

Yes, you're an expert. Don't fix co-workers cars or computers, and don't put an addition on your cousin's house. If anything goes wrong, you'll be to blame. The person who had the work done will be the victim, and you, the expert, will be the criminal. Therefore, if you know how to program websites and the subject comes up at work, stick a donut in your mouth…a big one.

> "There is not one wise man in twenty
> who will praise himself"
> ~ *William Shakespeare*

53. Tell the world you found a bag of money

Never, ever, ever share the fact that you found some cash, won the lottery, or came into an inheritance. If you have any long lost relatives, this is a sure fire way to find them; or rather they'll find you.

The sticky part of broadcasting to the world that you came into some money is you will be forever marked as wealthy. Even if it's only a few thousand dollars, if you ever try to pitch to someone at a later date that money is tight, they will say, "but I thought you got all that money". As soon as people think you have cash, they think you have too much. Therefore, if you win the lottery, just go to work like nothing happened.

"Well timed silence hath more eloquence than speech"
~ *Martin Fraquhar Tupper*

54. Argue with people who are impossible

There are certain people in this world who are totally impossible. This is what they like to do, and they're good at it to boot. Somehow, some of us lost souls continue to bring ideas, opinions and concepts to impossible people somehow expecting them to be reasonable this time. Go find a brick wall and bang your thick head on it. You'll make more progress.

"It is impossible to defeat an ignorant man in an argument"
~ *William G. McAdoo*

55. Help other people first

This is a total waste of time, although I must admit I've done it. You're not going to get anywhere giving free business classes to friends and relatives. You certainly need to have concern for others, but get yourself straightened out first.

It's difficult to resist volunteering an inordinate amount of your life coaching others after you've had a small success. You don't have to be a jerk, but don't lose sight of your totally selfish goal. You want to have a bunch of cash so you can buy a nifty car or an airplane and make a movie if you feel like it. Wait until you're filthy rich and then start in with the intellectual philanthropy.

> "Advice is judged by results, not by intentions"
> ~ *Cicero (106-43 B.C.)*

Backward - (most books just have a Forward)

View life from the inside out. View business from the outside in. Everything in life is understood from your viewpoint, and everything in business must be analyzed from everyone else's.

Before you do anything, figure out exactly what you want. You may want a house, a horse, a car, or an airplane. Write it down and frame it, so you can look at it every day.

Then figure out what everyone else wants. This is the key to business. Nobody cares about you. They want what they want.

Failure is information; fear is just a theory. Nothing goes as planned. Whenever you start a new project, expect it to feel like six picture puzzles poured into one box. Links in the chain of success are never assembled in a straight line.

"Failures blame other people, while the successful
can only blame themselves"
~ Eric Polster

Appendix 1 – Recommended reading

1) Franklin, Benjamin. - *The Way to Wealth*
This book has been in print for more than two hundred years. Need I say more…

2) Fox, Jeffrey J. - *How to become CEO*
Crisp and to the point. Excellent read.

3) Kiyosaki, Robert T. & Lechter, Sharon L. - *Rich Dad Poor Dad*
This book discusses financial literacy that is not taught in school.

4) Levinson, Jay Conrad & Godin, Seth. - *The Guerilla Marketing Handbook*
This book is an extensive collection of marketing ideas and angles.

5) Tzu, Sun - *The Art of War*
This book is required reading for the Russian Army. This book is the most influential study of strategy ever written. Strategy of war applies directly to strategy in business.

6) Stanley, Thomas J. – *The Millionaire Next Door*
There are seven rules to becoming rich, and every rich person knows what they are. All seven are in this book.

www.ingramcontent.com/pod-product-compliance
Lightning Source LLC
Chambersburg PA
CBHW021957290426
44108CB00012B/1107